Billy Millie & TROY

Written and Illustrated

by

Copyright © 2017 by Jasmine Davis.

Jasmine Davis/The Awakening Remnant
ellipsesarts@gmail.com

Ordering Information:
Quantity sales. Special discounts are available on quantity purchases by corporations, associations, and others. For details, contact the "Special Sales Department" at the email address above.
Billy, Millie, and Troy/ Jasmine Davis —1st ed.
ISBN 978-0-9986926-2-3

Dedication

I dedicate this book to my husband Stephen. You are the peanut butter to my jelly, the banana to my smoothie, and the chips to my salsa. I love you through inifinity. Thank you for sharing your life with me.

-J.C.D.

"Whoever pursues righteousness and love finds life, prosperity, and honor"

Proverbs 21:21

Once upon a time there was an egg on a leaf, with no parents around, who knew what it could be.
That night a mighty wind came, and blew all the leaves far away.

Early that morning, when the wind was no longer blowing, the leaf gently laid to rest and covered a hole, an inch at best.

"Hey who turned out the light?" said Billy in a fright.
"Not me" said Mille his wife, "there's a leaf blocking the light.

So they climbed to move the leaf, and the egg they did see. And in that instant he knew, a father he would be.

"AAAAwwww," said Millie as her heart started to warm.
"This poor little egg was out in the storm."

wiggle

Wiggle

wiggle

Wiggle

"Whooh!! Look, did you see? It's about to hatch, oh lucky me."
"I suppose you want to keep him. I can see it in your eyes. Come on, bring him in, get him out of bird's site."
So she held him in her arms, keeping him nice and warm, hoping today was the day they would finally have their babe.

"He's here, he's here!" she said
overjoyed.
"Come quick to meet our new son
Troy."
"Look at all those colors on this
small little guy. He is truly special,
a gift from the Most High."
As the days went by, he grew up as
their own, a gift from above that
was brought by the storm.

POP!

Later that year, it became very clear,
that the birds from the south were
unpleasantly near.
"Son, the birds are back in town,
spreading fear all around.
So it's time for me to tell you,
we are first on their menu.
So keep low underground,
where you'll be safe and sound."

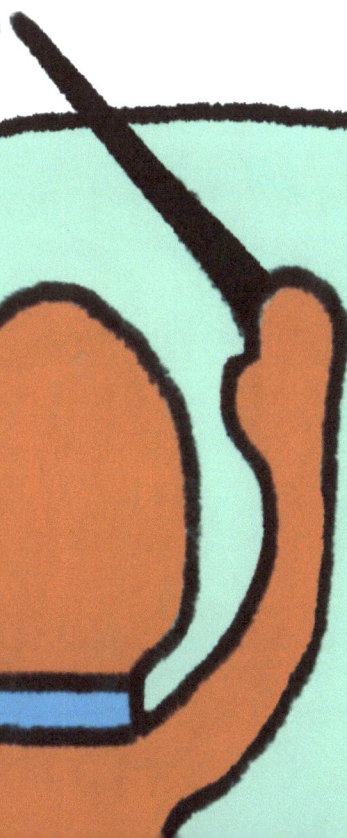

The news of danger worried the little worm, the poor little guy couldn't help but squirm.

"I know I know, I need a place to hide that's just big enough, for me to fit inside.

So the little worm started building, and his parents thought it to be strange, but little did they know he was entering a new stage.

So the days went by, and his parents did wait, for that bright, early morning of the 26th day.

wiggle wiggle

wiggle wiggle

Wiggle

"He's back, he's back our son
is back, but he sure looks
different, and that's a fact."
"I knew you were special
and not a worm at all,
for one you have feet, and
us, we crawl."
"You are a butterfly,
beautiful too, and because
you can fly I know just
what to do."

So Billy went away and began weaving, for he now had a plan for the way they'd be leaving.

"I've made a basket that is to be lifted, that is just big enough for us to fit in. And with those big wings, you can now fly, to a place I have dreamed of all of my life."

So they packed what they needed and off they went, to the place where his father had always dreamt.

"This is it, this is it, the place I had dreamed, and it truly is all I thought it would be.
A place for you and a place for me, with good soft ground and big tall trees.
We've made it here, to a garden you see, where we can live our lives happily, bird free!"

THE

END

www.ingramcontent.com/pod-product-compliance
Lightning Source LLC
LaVergne TN
LVHW072055070426
835508LV00002B/103